FUN WITH
HISTORICAL COSTUME

by Valerie Janitch

KAYE & WARD · LONDON
in association with Hicks, Smith & Sons
Australia and New Zealand

First published by
KAYE & WARD LTD
21 New Street, London EC2M 4NT
1975

ISBN 0 7182 0092 6

Printed in England by Whitstable Litho,
Straker Brothers Ltd, Whitstable.

Acknowledgements

The publishers wish to thank the following for
permission to reproduce photographs in this book:
The Victoria and Albert Museum for the picture on the
title page and those on pages 4 (bottom) 22, 50, 51, 56
57 and 62; The British Library Board for pictures on
pages 4 (top) and 17; pictures on pages 3 and 16 are
reproduced by courtesy of the Trustees of the National
Gallery, London; page 6 by permission of Manchester
City Art Gallery; page 63 by permission of Leeds City
Art Gallery; page 34 by permission of The National
Portrait Gallery, London; pages 23, 28, 29 and 35 by
permission of Sotheby & Co; and the Gainsborough
portraits from The Queen's Gallery on pages 44 and 45
by gracious permission of Her Majesty the Queen.
Photographs of Miss Janitch's collages on pages 9, 13,
19, 25, 31, 37, 41, 47, 53 and 59 were taken by Angelo
Hornak.

Contents

Introduction

This book sets out to do two things. To outline the fascinating history of fashion from the Middle Ages to the end of the last century – and to show you the equally fascinating craft of collage. So when you have finished the book, not only will you know how costume has developed over a period of six centuries, but you can also be the owner of an attractive set of collage pictures to display on your walls.

You will see that the colours of the fabrics and papers used for the collages illustrated are always described in the directions. This is partly because the colours of the fashions are chosen as typical of that particular period – and also because the combination contrasts with, and shows up well against, the background shade suggested. In the same way, the surround is always chosen to compliment and emphasize the colours of the design. But you don't *have* to be guided by the examples shown here: you can substitute alternative colour schemes and fabrics to suit your own taste, or to fit in with what you have available. And of course, you don't have to do the collages in fabric – you *could* make them in paper .... and you might prefer to compose an impressive album, to illustrate the history of fashion, by pasting them into a scrap book.

(*Title page*). One of the periods when "fashion" reached such exaggerated extremes that it appeared ridiculous and unpractical. This fashion print of 1798 shows clearly the outline of the basket-like panniers tied at each side of the waist to hold the skirt out over the hips. The gown, which has a train at the back, is trimmed with heavy embroidery and extravagantly frilled with ruffled lace: lace and ribbons again form part of the complicated grey-powdered hairstyle, which is topped with an enormous ostrich plume. Once a style reached such proportions that it became unmanageable and ugly, it heralded the beginning of something new – which was usually a complete contrast, much simpler and far more elegant. (*Victoria and Albert Museum. Crown Copyright*)

(*Above*). Portrait of a Woman by Lucas Cranach the Elder. This portrait of a German woman in the first half of the sixteenth century shows the emergence of the dress in the shape that we know it today. Bodice, waist, sleeves and skirt all follow the line of the body, instead of all or part of it being obscured by loose folds of drapery. A picture like this would make an ideal subject for a collage: you could use different braids and ribbons for the bands on the sleeves, tiny jewels for her necklace and rings, fine cord to criss-cross her waist – and minute beads and seed pearls to pick out the pattern on her bodice and for her headdress. Stranded embroidery cotton soaked in wallpaper paste would make her fair hair, and you could twist gilt picture wire to reproduce the heavy gold chain round her shoulders. (*Reproduced by courtesy of the Trustees, The National Gallery, London*)

3

(*Above right*). Dame Nature gives her orders to Genius, taken from *Roman de la Rose*. Harley, MS. 4425, f.166
The British Library.
A medieval lady wearing a mantle over her cotehardie and surcote. Her reticulated headdress is an elaborate framework of gold, filled in with finely worked gold mesh interlaced with velvet and decorated with jewels. The man's hood was called a chaperon: he could wind the long end round and round his head to make a fashionable hat – or round his neck to keep him warm.

(*Below right*). A dress for taking a walk in 1840. In the early years of Queen Victoria's reign, skirts were held out in a bell shape over several layers of stiff petticoats. Waists were tiny and emphasized by a wide V-shaped neckline. Buttons, bows, braid and lace trimmed the gown – whilst the deep-brimmed poke bonnet was so heavily decorated that the actual shape was almost entirely lost in a profusion of ribbons, ruching, lace flounces and rosebuds. To complete the outfit, she carries an embroidered shawl with a fringed edge. (*Victoria and Albert Museum. Crown Copyright*)

About the Collages

If you have never done fabric collage before there are just a few things it will help you to know before you begin work on your first picture. Techniques to use for each design are individually covered in the text, and those recommended for the first designs are described in detail. Even if you don't plan to start with one of the first costumes, do read through the instructions so that you will learn the methods employed for the succeeding collages.

In each case, you will see that the directions tell you to trace the outline on to **Vilene.** This is a non-woven interfacing material, and although you *can* substitute paper if you wish, you will find it much easier, and achieve a far more satisfactory result, if you use Vilene. It is only semi-opaque white, and you should find you can see to trace through it without difficulty. Medium-weight is best for the majority of purposes: where light-weight is specified, it is because it is more suitable for that particular job–but it won't matter if you haven't any, use the medium-weight instead.

Black cartridge paper is used for the heads and arms or hands. This directs emphasis on the fashions–and avoids having to draw or paint faces and features!

Don't use very thin **fabrics** for the costumes, as the adhesive may tend to soak through and show on the right side. Try to find fabrics with a little body–a number of the collages illustrated are made from curtain fabrics cut from a sample colour swatch (you can often get out-of-date swatches from shops which specialize in soft furnishing fabrics, or make up curtains professionally). Felt is very easy to use, but does not give such an interesting effect for garments supposedly made from rich fabrics.

Look for the narrowest **braids and laces** you can find: stores that sell the silk and metallic fancy braids for dress and lampshade trimmings are your best hunting grounds.

Sometimes you can cut a narrow braid down the centre to make two lengths half the original width (look at the collages illustrated, and you will see how often this has been done with one particular kind of braid which was $\frac{1}{4}$ inch wide before it was cut–the mid-Victorian costume on page 53 shows it cut in half to trim the flounces, but used full width along the hem). Similarly, search for the tiniest beads, seed pearls and diamanté available, to make effective **jewellery**.

Use **fabric adhesive** when sticking fabric and paper to the Vilene, and for adding lace, braid, etcetera–but use an **all-purpose clear adhesive** for the non-porous things like beads, pearls, metal and so on: this is also good for mounting down, as the clear adhesive dries a little more slowly, and so allows you more time than the quick-drying fabric adhesive. Both these adhesives are "flexible", which is a great advantage and gives a far more satisfactory result–unlike the hard, brittle glue which was used for early collage work. **Wallpaper paste** is best for preparing the backgrounds: mix it to a quite thick consistency, and brush it over the surface smoothly but generously.

Finally, use an **invisible tape** with a matt surface to join the sections of Vilene together again after you have covered them: don't use the more usual, shiny kind of clear tape, but the type which is intended for mending torn paper, which has a dull finish on which it is possible to write. Use short lengths, stuck to the back of the Vilene.

The **mounts** used for the collages in this book were originally 12 inch square papier mâché cake stands–the kind which are sold covered with silver paper for wedding and birthday cakes. You can, of course, use any firm, flat mount to make the pictures: wood, heavy card, hardboard, etcetera. However, the cake stands are ideal because they are comparatively inexpensive, stay absolutely flat and do not bend or curl—and although quite light, are thick and heavy enough to make a picture without needing any additional backing or framing. If you plan to follow my example and use cake boards too, this is how they should be prepared.

First cut your board to size, using a sharp knife and a metal-edged rule (this should be done by a grown-up). Then smooth the surface with fine sandpaper, to remove the shiny sparkle of the silver paper (if you don't do this, the paste may not adhere properly). Now paste the surface and lay a piece of plain white tissue paper over it, smoothing the tissue down flat and allowing it to overlap the sides about 2 inches all round: then take this excess neatly round and stick it to the back (cut away a triangle at each corner before doing so). This will give you a perfectly smooth surface on which to paste your background paper, and will also neaten the sides of your board (otherwise the papier mâché composition may tend to crumble where you have cut the stand).

Now cover your mount with **background paper** and a surround, as illustrated. Choose a background colour against which your collage will stand out clearly: it is best to complete your figure to the stage of mounting down before finally deciding on your background shade (the colours stated in the book are indicated for guidance in choosing suitable contrasts)—then try the figure against different alternatives to see the effect.

To make a picture the same size as the ones in this book, cut your background paper the same size as your mount (12 inches by 9½ inches). Paste the paper thoroughly, and rest it gently in position on the mount, making sure the edges are level before smoothing it firmly all over with a clean soft cloth or paper towel, to remove any air bubbles which may be trapped underneath.

Leave this to dry while you decide the colour of your **surround**, if you have not already done so. This should be a distinct contrast to

(*Above*). A beautiful gown of silk brocade made in the 1740's, which has survived to the present day. The cream silk is heavily embroidered with an all-over pattern of delicate pink, blue, yellow and white flowers, with softly shaded leaves in green and golden brown. The dress is split right down the front to form an "open robe" revealing the separate stomacher which is again embroidered, this time on a green ground. Below this would be worn a contrasting underskirt. It isn't always easy to find brocades thin enough, and with a small design suitable for collage (if the pattern is too big for the scale, it will look out of proportion, and the effect will be wrong). Alternatively, look out for printed gift-wrapping papers: they can often provide a surprisingly successful substitute – at a very modest price!

the background paper, and preferably either tone with and echo the colour of the costume, or pick out one of the colours which appear in the design. Cut this paper exactly the same size as the first piece. Then rule a line 1 inch from the edge all round (measure this very carefully, as it must be absolutely accurate). Finally, cut along each line with a sharp knife and metal-edged rule, making sure the corners where the lines meet are clean and neat. Paste the surround and lay it gently over the background paper, edges level, as before: then smooth firmly into place. If the surround is not sticking properly at any point, don't be afraid to lift it gently and brush some more paste underneath: any paste which appears on the surface can be wiped away, and won't leave a mark when it dries.

When the picture is quite finished, you can either leave it as it is—or add a **frame** of decorative braid as shown in the illustrations.

One of the great advantages about the craft of collage is the fact that so little **equipment** is necessary—all of which you will probably have. Scissors are most important—a large pair is very useful, but a small, pointed pair is essential: these must be sharp with well-aligned blades, so that they cut cleanly and accurately. A well-sharpened pencil, a ruler (preferably with a metal edge—otherwise you will also need a piece of straight metal to cut against), a craft knife (the "Olfa", which has snap-off blades, is ideal), pins and occasionally a needle—and the adhesives previously mentioned, together with a thick brush (about 1 inch wide) for the paste, and a spreader for the fabric adhesive (this usually comes with the tube): choose a clear adhesive which has a long, pointed nozzle, so that you can apply it direct—or use a pin when applying it to very small areas.

One final word of advice before you begin. Collage is easy and great fun—but above all, remember that care and accuracy are essential for a really successful, professional-looking finish. Work slowly and carefully, cutting the fabric absolutely level with the edge of the Vilene (if the fabric tends to fray, spread a little adhesive on the wrong side beyond the edge of the Vilene shape). Then tape the sections together again with the edges exactly matching, placing the pieces over the pattern to determine the correct position. As long as you are accurate and neat, read and understand the directions before you begin, and then follow them in the right order, you can be sure of a collage which will be admired by all who see it!

Medieval Beginnings

The first collage depicts a Medieval costume of about 1250-1300. Until this time, clothes had been very practical – loosely draped garments held in by a girdle at the waist, with a mantle (cloak) over the top. In other words, they were sensible, easy-to-wear and – above all, warm. But during the thirteenth century, the wealthy nobles at court gradually began to take an interest in fashion, and by about 1300, definite styles had developed. Rich new fabrics had been brought back from the East by returning Crusaders, and these were decorated or trimmed with fur to make much more tailored garments than had ever been known before.

This trend began, surprisingly, with men. But women soon copied the fitted styles which their menfolk had adopted, and began wearing a gown with a high neck, tight sleeves and closely fitting bodice, called a cotehardie. The sleeves were buttoned from elbow to wrist, and the back was laced. Low round the hips was a broad belt made of metal, and elaborately jewelled.

Soon women took to wearing another garment over the fitted gown. They called it a super-cotehardie – or surcote. This over-gown was much looser, with a very full skirt: but it had a wide neck and enormous sleeveless armholes, which revealed the cotehardie and jewelled girdle beneath. It was often edged with fur, and had a row of buttons down the centre front, ending at the waist.

For extra warmth, they added a very full mantle, which was loosely draped over the shoulders and fastened at the top by cords across the front, so that it hung down in flowing folds at the back. It was often lined with fur.

Women had always covered their hair with linen scarves and veils: however, now they began to dress their hair in elaborate styles – enclosing plaits at each side of the face in jewelled gold nets (called crispines) – or wearing a coif or fillet low over the forehead, with all the hair held by a crispine. But many women still clung to the old-fashioned wimple – which was a white linen scarf draped round the head and held in place by a chin band of the same material. In our picture the lady wears an elaborate gold coif or fillet over her wimple: but the coif might just as well have been in plain white too.

Early Medieval: 1250-1300

Materials:
Medium-weight Vilene
Light-weight Vilene
Light olive green fabric for cotehardie
Blue felt for surcote
White felt for wimple
Narrow gold or decorative braid for girdle
Gold braid (or white or gold paper) for coif
Very narrow brown braid to trim surcote
Very tiny gilt beads for sleeve buttons
Slightly larger gilt beads for surcote buttons
Small blue glass beads for belt jewels (optional)
Black paper for face and hands
Cream paper for background
Light olive paper for surround
Cake board or alternative mount 12in by
9$\frac{1}{2}$in
$\frac{1}{4}$ yd braid to frame (optional)
Scotch "Magic" invisible tape
Polycell wallpaper paste
Copydex fabric adhesive
Evo-stik clear adhesive

Method: Trace the figure on to medium-weight Vilene, then cut all round the outer edge very carefully.

Now cut off the head–across the broken line A-A. And cut off the hands along the bottoms of the sleeves–B-B.

Stick the *right side* of the Vilene head to the *back* of your black paper. Do the same with the hands. When dry, cut out these three pieces, following the edge of the Vilene very carefully.

Mark the broken line C-C on the figure. Spread adhesive over the whole figure above this line–then press down on the back of your green (cotehardie) fabric. When dry, cut all the surplus fabric away, following the shape of the Vilene figure.

Place the head and figure face down, meeting exactly edge-to-edge: hold carefully together and join with invisible tape. Replace the hands

at the bottom of the arms in the same way.

Place your figure over the pattern, and mark the position of the girdle at each side (the lines have been extended so that you can do this). Stick a short piece of narrow gold or decorative braid across the hips at each side, following the pattern: allow the cut ends to overlap at each side, and at the centre, as indicated by the broken lines. Fold the overlapping ends at the sides round to the back and stick.

Now make a paper pattern for the surcote by tracing it from the pattern. Cut out your tracing and pin it to your blue felt–then cut out neatly. If you like, you can leave a little extra on all the edges which form *the edge of the figure* (the cut edge of the Vilene)– and cut them away level with the Vilene when the felt is mounted down. Spread adhesive over the back of the felt, then press carefully down into position on the figure.

Stick very narrow braid round the neck and armhole edges of the surcote, as illustrated.

Trace the wimple–in one piece–on to light-weight Vilene. Then turn your Vilene over and mark the outline again on the back. Stick the *right* side of the Vilene to the back of your white felt. When it is dry, cut very carefully round the line on the back of the Vilene. Stick into position on the head, making sure the outer edges of the felt and figure are exactly matching.

Stick gold braid (or white or gold paper) across the top of the head for the coif–trimming level with the edges.

Prepare your mount as already described (pages 5 & 6), and paste cream paper over the entire surface for the background. Then cut the surround as explained on page 6, and paste that carefully into place.

Place the figure on the background to decide the best position. When you are satisfied, mark the top corners of the head, tips of the hands and corners of the hem. Then remove the

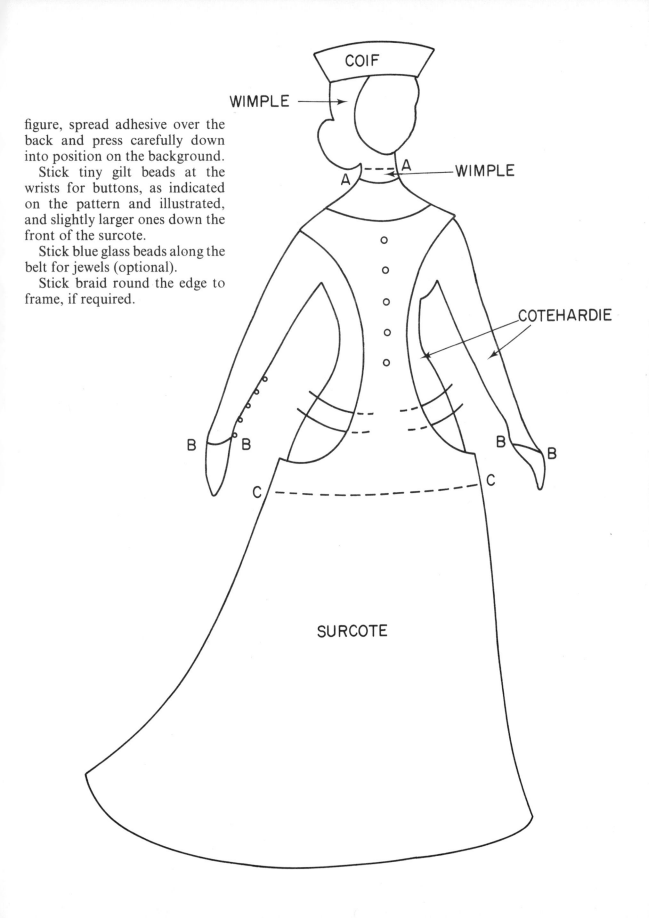

figure, spread adhesive over the back and press carefully down into position on the background.

Stick tiny gilt beads at the wrists for buttons, as indicated on the pattern and illustrated, and slightly larger ones down the front of the surcote.

Stick blue glass beads along the belt for jewels (optional).

Stick braid round the edge to frame, if required.

COIF

WIMPLE

WIMPLE

A

A

COTEHARDIE

B B

B B

C C

SURCOTE

Late Medieval Elegance

Noble ladies now began to follow fashion very seriously, and by the middle of the fifteenth century were vying with each other in the splendour of their brocades, the luxury of their fur trimmings and the height of their elaborate headdresses. Having at last revealed the shape of their figure, after so many centuries of heavily draped garments, women were anxious to show it off to the best advantage. And so the fashions which developed were elegant and beautiful.

The new gown was called a houppelande. This was, in origin, the cotehardie–which you will remember had long, tight sleeves and a fitted bodice. But the houppelande had a very wide and low V or U shaped neckline– *so* low that it had to be filled in with a tiny "modesty vest" at its lowest point–and the waistline was very high, marked by a broad, jewelled belt pushed right up under the bust. From this fell a very full skirt, which lengthened at the back into a wide train. The hem of the gown was edged with fur–and there would usually be more fur bordering the neckline and wrist edges of the long sleeves.

Once again the hair was hidden: so much so, that any stray hairs which might be visible on the forehead or neck were quickly plucked out! Headdresses were so varied and so ima-ginative that it is almost impossible to give a general description. The first were very wide, and usually "reticulated" (made of metal mesh), enclosing the hair. Often they were horn-shaped–curving out and up at each side of the head: these horns would be draped with a wide veil which fell over the face and down at the sides and back. Sometimes they were vast jewelled turbans, swathed in silk. Or they could be heart-shaped–again draped with a veil. Whatever their shape, they were usually made of gold, with velvet or silk, and heavily decorated with jewels and ropes of pearls.

Then, about the middle of the fifteenth century, headdresses became narrower and taller–and the hennin appeared. This had several shapes, but the most popular was the steeple–like the one in our collage. It was covered in brocade, and had a folded band of black velvet across the front, which hung down in "lappets" at the sides of the head. Over the entire hennin was draped a long, filmy veil, sometimes ground-length, which hung down at the back. In later years the hennin became shorter–as if its point had been cut off half-way down–and this was often worn with a veil draped over two or three up-standing wires, so that it hung in a butterfly shape.

Late Medieval: 1450

Materials:
Medium-weight Vilene
Light-weight Vilene
Purple fabric for houppelande
Silver-grey patterned brocade for undergown
  and hennin
Scrap of embroidered ribbon or fabric for
  frontlet
¾in wide white velvet ribbon to edge gown
Black velvet or velvet ribbon for lappets
Narrow gold braid for belt
Tiny seed pearls and coloured glass beads for
  belt (optional)
White tissue paper for veil
Black paper for face and hand
Deep yellow paper for background
Mid blue paper for surround
Cake board or alternative mount 12in by
  9½in
1¼yd braid to frame (optional)
Black fibre-tipped or felt pen
Scotch "Magic" invisible tape
Polycell wallpaper paste
Copydex fabric adhesive
Evo-stik clear adhesive

Method: Trace the whole figure—except for
the veil—on to medium-weight Vilene, then
cut all round the outer edge very carefully.
Now, on a separate piece of Vilene, trace the
arm and hand again, and cut this out too.

Cut away the head as before–including the
lappets and frontlet: to do this, follow lines
A-A and B-B-B. Cut the hand off the *separate*
arm, along line C-C.

Stick the right side of the Vilene head and
hand to the back of your paper and, when dry,
cut out as you did before.

Cut away the undergown along line D-D:
but before doing so, mark the point where the
undergown joins the houppelande on the
back of the Vilene–as indicated by the arrow.

Cover the undergown and hennin with
brocade in the usual way, carefully trimming
the edge of the fabric level with the Vilene.

Cut the Vilene hand off the figure (along
C-C) and throw it away. Then cover the whole
remaining figure with purple fabric. Cover
the separate arm in the same way.

When you have done this, carefully tape
the head back on to the figure, the hennin on
to the head, the undergown to the houppelande and the hand to the separate arm–
always making sure the pieces are in exactly
the correct position, with the edges matching
and level.

Stick a tiny piece of embroidered ribbon or
fabric across for the frontlet–trimming it
level with the edge of the Vilene, but allowing
it slightly to overlap the edge of the gown (but
not beyond the broken line).

Cut each side edge off some white velvet
ribbon to make it the correct width to edge the
neckline and cuff–as indicated by the broken
lines. Allow it to overlap the front of the
figure, turning the surplus round and sticking
to the back, but trim level with the back edge
of the figure. Overlap each edge of the wrist,
and fold cut ends round to the back.

Stick gold braid into position for the belt–
overlapping in front and folding round to the
back as above, but only as far as indicated
by the broken lines on the arm.

Stick white velvet ribbon along the lower
edge of the houppelande, folding the end
round to the back in front, but trimming level
with the edge of the hem at the back, as illustrated.

Carefully stick the separate arm into position
on the figure.

Trace the lappets on to light-weight Vilene–
turn over and trace through to the back. Stick
the right side of the Vilene to the back of your
black velvet (spread the adhesive on the fabric),
and when dry, cut out. Stick into position on
the figure.

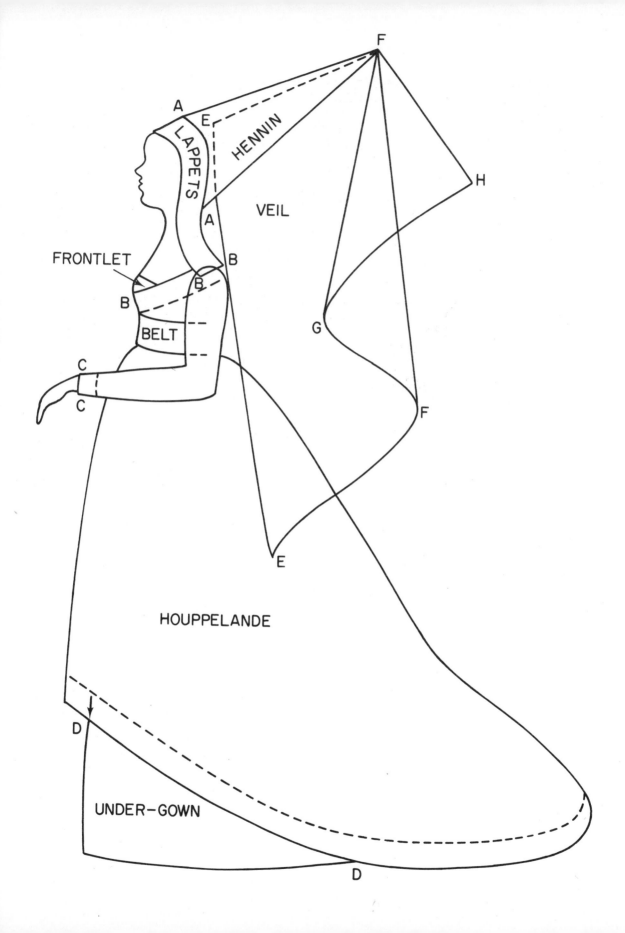

16

Prepare your mount and paste deep yellow paper over the entire surface for the background, followed by a mid-blue surround (see pages 5 and 6).

Place the figure on the background to decide the best position. When you are satisfied, mark the point of the hennin, the tip of the hand, the front and back of the hem of the houppelande and the front corner of the undergown. Then remove the figure, spread adhesive over the back *leaving the hennin free,* and press carefully down into position on the background.

Now make the veil, tracing it on to white tissue paper as follows. First trace the section which falls between the lines E-E and F-F – extending it up to the broken lines. Cut out and paste (using wallpaper paste) carefully into position, the top section underneath the hennin as indicated on the pattern. Now trace the section which falls between the lines F-G and F-F: cut out and paste into position, over the previous piece. Finally, trace the section between F-G and F-H: cut this out and paste down as before. Now stick the hennin into place.

Stick tiny seed pearls along each side of the belt, with coloured glass beads decorating the centre of the gold braid.

Mark the velvet into "ermine" with a felt pen, as illustrated.

Stick braid round the edge to frame, if required.

(*Above*). A late fifteenth century representation of the marriage between King Louis of Naples and Sicily to Princess Yolande of Aragon taken from Froissart's Chronicle. Harley MS 4379, f. 12b. (The British Library). The princess is watched by her ladies, whom she has brought with her from Spain: all wear the fashionable cotehardie, lifted to reveal a contrasting underskirt – their hair hidden beneath tall steeple hennins.

(*Left*). Detail from The Virgin and Child with Saints by Hans Memling, reproduced by courtesy of The National Gallery, London.
A lovely painting of an elegant Medieval lady holding her prayer book, showing the fashionable very wide, low neckline filled in with a frontlet above the high waist marked by a broad belt. Her tightly fitting sleeves are so long that they extend over her hands – and she wears an abbreviated hennin without a point, over which is draped a filmy veil. Notice how the little girl wears a dress very similar to her mother's – and that she has identical black velvet lappets draped over her head and shoulders, but without the hennin behind.

17

Tudor Change

By the middle of the sixteenth century, dress had changed almost completely. Women still wore an underskirt of rich material–called a kirtle–but instead of lifting the hem of the overgown to show it, the skirt was split right down the centre front to reveal a triangular area of the beautiful fabric beneath.

The shape of the gown was quite different, too. Corsets were introduced, to give a long, slender figure–which was emphasized by the tightly fitted bodice, pointed waistline and bell-like skirt (which was held out by a cone-shaped stiffened canvas petticoat under the kirtle).

Fabrics were rich and beautiful–and the fashions were designed to use them as lavishly as possible. This is particularly noticeable in the sleeves–which again belled out from a fitted top and emphasized the slim waistline: these sleeves were so wide that they were folded back over the lower part of the arm to show a false under-sleeve beneath. The wide, hanging sleeve of the gown would have a rich lining–and often the under-sleeve would be "slashed"–to look as if it had been cut by a sword–and "puffed", with a contrasting fabric underneath which would show through when the slits were pulled open. This "slashing and puffing" was very fashionable at this time, and appeared all over men's clothes.

Necklines were square–very low and very wide. Women wore a chemise–which was similar to a man's shirt–under their gown, and the lace edge of this was just visible at the neckline and wrists.

The hair was held in a black velvet bag, which hung down at the back of the head. The "gable hood" was the most popular head-dress at this time. It was usually very elaborate, made of gold and precious stones. Later came the very flattering horse-shoe shaped "French hood", worn far back on the head, revealing the hair in front.

Ladies usually wore a pomander suspended on a chain round their waists: this was a jewelled case like a small round box, which was perforated, and held sweet-scented perfumes, herbs or spices. This was not only pleasant, but necessary, as personal cleanliness was not considered very important–and the streets were littered with piles of refuse, causing bad smells and very serious danger of infection.

Tudor: 1540

Materials:
Medium-weight Vilene
Deep crimson velvet for the gown
Cream and gold brocade for kirtle and sleeve
    linings
Dark, patterned fabric for sleeves
Rose satin or satin ribbon for slashings
Narrow white lace for cuffs and neck
Very narrow matching braid for the gown
Narrow gold braid for headdress
Tiny gilt beads for necklaces and pomander
Amber and emerald diamantés or beads for
    necklace and pomander
Tiny seèd pearls for headdress
Green glass beads for headdress (optional)
Black paper for face and hands
Deep yellow paper for headdress
Pale green paper for background
Wine-coloured paper for surround
Cake board or alternative mount 12in by
    9½in
1¼yd braid to frame (optional)
Scotch "Magic" invisible tape
Polycell wallpaper paste
Copydex fabric adhesive
Evo-stik clear adhesive

Method: Trace the whole figure on to medium-weight Vilene, then cut round the outer edge very carefully (you can remove the sections between arms and body later). Now trace the head on to Vilene again, including the head-dress, but ending at the broken line which crosses the face. Cut out. Finally, trace each undersleeve and hand (ignoring the broken lines indicating lace at the wrists), and cut these out too.

First, cover the separate Vilene head and headdress with deep yellow paper, trimming level with the edge in the usual way.

Now, on the main figure, cut away the face and shoulders, following the profile of the face on the left, the inner edge of the gable head-dress, and the neckline of the dress. Cover with black paper in the usual way. (Keep the cut-away Vilene headdress for later). Cut the hands off the *separate* sleeves and cover these with black paper too.

Place the yellow paper-covered head exactly over the pattern on page 21: then stick the black covered face on top, matching the chin and the neckline on the pattern below, to ensure the position is absolutely accurate.

Turn the two separate under-sleeves over, and trace the two "slashes" on each through to the back. Then cover the front with your under-sleeve fabric (this can be the same as the kirtle, with a different fabric for the sleeve linings) in the usual way. When the under-sleeves are quite dry, cut out the two "slashes" very carefully (as it is best to do this with a sharp craft knife, it might be wise to ask a grown-up to help here). Then stick a piece of rose satin to the back of the under-sleeve, behind the slashes, so that the right side of the satin shows through.

Stick the hands back into place against the under-sleeves with invisible tape. Cut two lace cuffs, as indicated by the broken lines on the pattern, and stick into place.

Stick the top edge of a strip of lace along the lower edge of the neckline on the paper-covered head, so that only a fraction will show (see illustration and broken line on pattern): trim off over-lapping lace all round.

Returning to the main figure, cut off the sleeve and sleeve lining at each side, following the broken lines indicating the edge of the skirt, and ignoring the under-sleeves completely (at the same time you can cut away the areas between the arms and body). Now cut away the *whole* sleeve lining on each piece – all the way up to the top, so that it includes the section of under-sleeve marked on it (the line to cut is marked A-A on one sleeve – cut

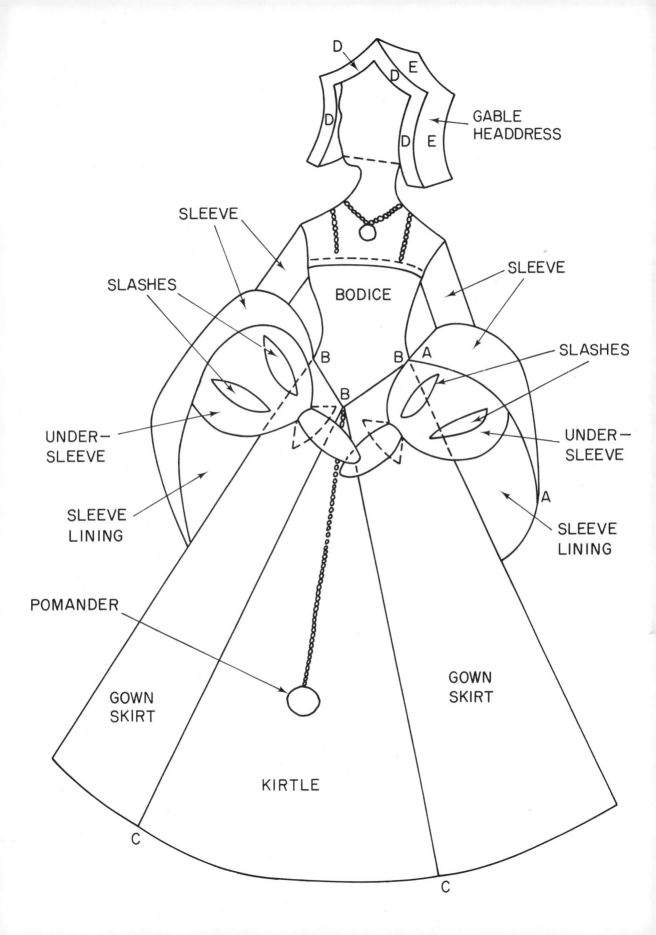

GABLE
HEADDRESS

SLEEVE

SLASHES

SLEEVE

BODICE

SLASHES

UNDER–
SLEEVE

UNDER–
SLEEVE

SLEEVE
LINING

SLEEVE
LINING

POMANDER

GOWN
SKIRT

GOWN
SKIRT

KIRTLE

the other sleeve in the same way). Cover these two sleeve lining pieces with cream brocade (or alternative: as mentioned previously, they do not have to be the same as the kirtle). And cover the two oddly-shaped sleeve pieces which remain, with velvet (spread fabric adhesive on the back of the velvet and then press the Vilene down on to it: when dry, cut out the Vilene shapes as usual, through the adhesive which extends beyond the edge. This will prevent the velvet fraying–and is a very satisfactory method of covering for all heavy fabrics which tend to fray). Join the sleeves

(Victoria and Albert Museum. Crown Copyright)

and sleeve linings together again with invisible tape at the back.

Now cut away the bodice along lines B-B-B.

(*Below*). Jacques de Savoie, Duc de Nemonts and Elizabeth of Austria. These French fashions of 1560–80 are more than twenty years later than the collage – yet you can see how little styles have changed. The most important new developments are the finely pleated, starched neck ruffs which were worn by both male and female alike – and the lady's very attractive French hood, which reveals far more hair than had ever been seen before. The detail sketches will help to give you some idea of the ornate jewellery popular at the time: this kind of detail is very useful when you are doing research for a collage, as it will make your design much more authentic – so always keep an eye open for it, and a sketchbook handy to make notes.

22

Cover with velvet. (Incidentally, the type used in the illustration is known as "crushed velvet", and has a rather uneven surface – which gives a most attractive effect, looking a little like cut velvet brocade).

Cut away each side of the gown skirt, along lines B-C, and cover these with velvet, too.

Cover the kirtle with brocade. Then tape the skirt and kirtle together again – joining the bodice at the top in the same way.

Tape the head to the top of the bodice, then tape the sleeves into position at each side, joining at the neck and sides of the skirt.

Stick very narrow matching braid down the inner edges of the skirt where it meets the kirtle (lines B-C).

Thread a length of tiny gilt beads down the centre front of the kirtle, between B and the pomander (secure each end of your cotton to the back of the Vilene). Stick additional lengths of threaded beads along the waistline dividing the bodice and skirt (B-B-B).

Stick the under-sleeves into position, over the sleeve linings and skirt, the hands overlapping as indicated.

Stick narrow braid round the lower edge of each sleeve, where it meets the under-sleeve and lining.

Thread tiny gilt beads between the neckline of the bodice and the shoulders, as indicated. Then stick an amber diamanté or bead in the centre, as shown, and add another string of beads at each side, so that it looks as if it is suspended from a necklace.

Prepare your mount and paste pale green paper over the entire surface for the background, followed by a wine-coloured surround (see pages 5 and 6).

Place the figure on the background, decide and mark the position, then stick down in the usual way.

To make the gable headdress, stick two rows of tiny seed pearls to the yellow paper to form the front (section marked D).

Now take the Vilene headdress which you cut away from the main figure, and cut off the back section marked E-E (discard D). Fit

(*Above*). Mary Tudor, Hans Eworth. A portrait of Mary Tudor painted in 1554. Although the square neckline was still worn, Mary favoured the new alternative – a high, up-standing collar lined with white lace and embroidered round the edge. Clusters of pearls decorate her French hood, and the intricate pattern on her kirtle and slashed under-sleeves is embroidered with countless more pearls. The long, hanging over-sleeves of her brocade gown are fur.

this over the yellow paper forming the back of the headdress and trim the inner edge if necessary. Then cover with gold braid – cutting the braid absolutely level with the edge of the Vilene. Stick into position, finishing with some coloured glass beads near the front, if liked (see illustration).

Stick an emerald diamanté or bead at the end of the pomander chain, and surround with a circle of gilt beads.

Stick braid round the edge to frame, if required.

Elizabethan Grandeur

English fashion has usually originated in – or at least been influenced by – Europe. This would often happen because the king married a foreign princess, and his new bride and her ladies would arrive wearing the latest fashions of their native country – which would then be eagerly copied by the ladies at court. Medieval clothes at the time of the Renaissance were influenced by Italy and sometimes France – Tudor costume followed the German styles of the Reformation : then Mary Tudor married Philip of Spain, and by Queen Elizabeth I's time, Spanish fashions led the way.

Corsets were now more rigid than ever, and must have been very uncomfortable to wear. The slender waistline had become so exaggerated that it was unnaturally elongated and ugly, and the richness of the fabrics, encrusted with jewels and decoration, became tasteless and ostentatious. This was a period of lavish over-ornamentation and extravagance – inspired and encouraged by the Queen, whose own wardrobe contained hundreds of dresses stiff with jewels and embroidery.

The farthingale petticoat began with the Spanish version, which had a padded roll round the hips, to hold the skirt out below the waist, with the canvas petticoat belling out below. But later the French farthingale became more popular: this had a wide hoop at the top, like a wheel, and the petticoat below hung straight down.

You can see this shape clearly in the collage: the skirt of the dress is stretched over the farthingale beneath, and then a separate circular frill, or ruff, rests on top round the hips.

Sleeves were now so enormous at the top that they had to be padded, but they fitted tightly at the wrist. This gave a very broad effect across the shoulders, which was emphasized by enormous lace ruffs and butterfly collars. Starch was introduced from Holland at this time, which made it possible to stiffen and pleat linen and lace in this way, and the fashion became very popular.

Jewels were worn at every possible place – long necklaces which hung below the waist, brooches, clasps, rings and headdresses – as well as being used in the embroidery of the clothes themselves. Queen Elizabeth was specially fond of pearls, and these are prominent in dresses of this period, as you can see if you study paintings of the Queen and ladies of the time.

One revolutionary new fashion could *not* be seen: knitted stockings replaced the fabric ones that had been worn before, and must have been far more comfortable. But they were severely frowned upon by many ladies, who considered them very daring, and refused to wear them!

Cosmetics were popular too, and the Queen painted her face more and more thickly the older she grew. She was famed for her white skin (she used a special almond cream, the recipe for which was a closely guarded secret), but the thick paint and vivid colours were quite unnatural, and looked almost mask-like.

Elizabethan: 1600

Materials:
Medium-weight Vilene
Light-weight Vilene
Silver-grey and yellow brocade for the dress
½in wide white lace for collar and cuffs (or
  alternative—see directions opposite)
Narrow white lace for neckline
Scrap of cream satin or ribbon or paper for fan
Very narrow golden yellow braid
Tiny gilt beads for necklace
Larger gilt beads for diadem headdress
Rose diamanté or bead for necklace
Amber diamanté and/or glass bead for diadem
Small oval or tear-drop pearl for headdress
Tiny seed pearls
Black paper for head and hands
Lilac paper for background
Grey paper for surround
Cake board or alternative mount 12in by
  9½in
1¼ yd braid to frame (optional)
Scotch "Magic" invisible tape
Polycell wallpaper paste
Copydex fabric adhesive
Evo-stik clear adhesive

Method: Trace the whole figure on to medium-weight Vilene, *except* for the right arm—follow the side of the neck (A-A) and the broken line indicating the edge of the skirt: ignore the fan, and the broken lines indicating the collar and cuffs. Now trace the right arm separately. Cut both pieces out very carefully.

Cut away the head along lines B-B and B-A. Cut off the hands at the wrists. Cover these three pieces with black paper in the usual way.

Stick the top edge of some narrow lace along the lower edge of the neckline (as broken line on pattern): trim away surplus overlap.

Cut the bodice along the curved waistline C-C-C, and then the skirt along the wavy line D-D. Cover the sleeves, bodice and two skirt pieces with brocade in the usual way.

Now tape all the pieces together again, adding the right arm.

Stick very narrow braid along the top edge of the bodice (B-A), round the waist (C-C-C) and along the wavy line joining the skirt (D-D). Stick a double width of braid along the hem.

Stick the lower part of the right arm down over the skirt.

Trace the collar on to light-weight Vilene from the separate pattern, and cut out.

Cut away the inner, straight edge of your ½ inch wide lace. Then stick or stitch the outer edge of the lace round the outer edge of the collar—slightly overlapping, and absolutely flat. When you have a row of lace all round the outer (scalloped) edge, stick the inner edge of the lace to the Vilene, gathering and folding it neatly and evenly so that it lies flat. Stick or stitch the outer edge of another row of lace so that it just overlaps the inner cut edge of the previous row: stick the inner edge neatly to the Vilene as before. Add a third row of lace in the same way.

Trim the neck edges of the collar to neaten, then stick into position as indicated by the broken lines on the pattern—slipping it behind the head and over each shoulder, and sticking in each place.

Cut lace to shape for the cuffs and stick into position as indicated. If you don't want to go to the trouble of making the collar as described, simply cut the shape from the pattern in a piece of lace of a suitable size, and stick into place just like the cuffs.

String tiny gilt beads round neck for the necklace, as indicated on the pattern.

Stick an oval or tear-drop pearl in the centre of the forehead, with a string of seed pearls at each side, as shown.

Prepare your mount and paste lilac paper over the entire surface for the background, followed by a grey surround (see pages 5, 6 and 7).

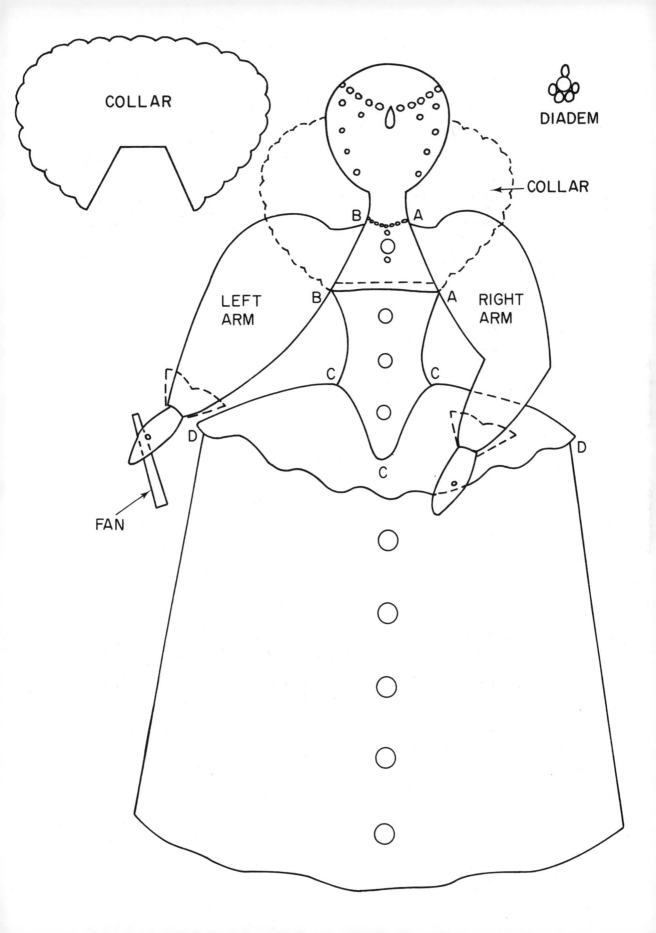

COLLAR

DIADEM

COLLAR

B A

LEFT
ARM

B A

RIGHT
ARM

C C

C

D

FAN

D

C

Place the figure on the background, decide and mark position, then stick down in the usual way – leaving the hand on the left free.

Trace the fan on to Vilene and cover with suitable fabric or paper. Then stick into position below the hand, and stick the hand down over it.

Stick short lengths of narrow braid into circles, to form rosettes – then stick down the front of the bodice and skirt as marked. Stick a seed pearl or similar decoration in the centre of each rosette.

Stick a tiny gilt bead below the centre of the necklace, with a rose diamanté or bead below it and a seed pearl below that.

Stick seed pearls over the sides of the head, as indicated and illustrated, and on the hands for rings.

Make up a tiny diadem on top of her head from gilt and glass beads, diamanté, etcetera, as illustrated (see separate diagram for composition of the diadem in the picture).

Stick braid round the edge to frame, if required.

The Elizabethan period is especially suitable for collage – and here are two subjects which would be ideal. They offer all the inspiration you need in the fly-away butterfly collars, the delicate lace cuffs, the rosettes, the long ropes of pearls, the necklaces, brooches, ear-rings and rings – and the jewelled hairstyles. If you can't find suitable brocades for the gowns, use plain fabrics, marking the low waist and hip-ruff with narrow braid – and perhaps even picking out a pattern in tiny beads on the contrasting kirtle and edging it with fringe before you stick it down. An unusual feature can be seen in the portrait of Queen Elizabeth: this is one of the rare periods in history when a woman's feet were visible – another opportunity to use your imagination and initiative with scraps of soft leather and jewelled buckles composed of tiny beads!

(*Left*). Portrait of Lady Clopton, Marcus Gheeraerts the Younger

(*Above*). Portrait of Elizabeth I, Marcus Gheeraerts the Younger

Stuart Naturalness

The Spanish Armada did nothing to enhance Spain in the eyes of England, and gradually the elaborate and stiff garments of Elizabeth's reign gave way in Stuart times to a softly feminine look which was both flattering and elegant. The figure resumed its natural shape, and plain fabrics relied on fullness, ruching and drapery to emphasise their beauty, instead of pattern and decorative embroidery. This change began when Anne of Austria, who was a leader of fashion, became Queen of France. Then Cavalier Charles I married a French queen, Henrietta Maria, who introduced the French fashions to the English court.

Rigid corsets disappeared, and stiff fabrics were replaced by beautiful silks, satins or velvets, falling in soft folds from a high waistline. A very full overskirt would be held up to reveal a contrasting skirt (or petticoat) beneath. Sleeves were equally full, but usually gathered at intervals so that they formed puffs round the arm, once more displaying the beauty of the fabric in the folds and gathers.

Lace and ribbons were used lavishly for decoration – but always emphasizing the softly draped and feminine effect. The Elizabethan high necks and starched ruffs were completely reversed: now deep collars formed by layers of exquisite lace fell from low, wide necklines which revealed the shoulders. More gathered lace was used for delicately flounced cuffs covering the forearm below the elbow-length sleeves. And everywhere – trimming necklines, bodices, sleeves, waists and skirts – ribbons were used to make bows, both large and small, rosettes and loops – a row of which often decorated the waistline.

Hairstyles followed the same pattern – soft curls framed the face, and ringlets fell loosely over the shoulders: a bun high on the back of the head would usually be decorated with a rope of pearls, or a ribbon bow – and pearls were the most popular choice of jewellery.

Stuart: 1640

Materials:
Medium-weight Vilene
Light-weight Vilene
Green fabric for the gown
Deep golden-yellow fabric for underskirt
$\frac{3}{4}$in wide white lace for collar and cuffs
Yellow satin or satin ribbon for bows
Very narrow greenish-gold braid for waist
Very tiny seed pearls for necklace and hair
Tiny seed pearl for ear-ring
Amber diamanté or bead for brooch
Tiny gilt beads to surround brooch (optional)
Black paper for head and hands
Pale pink paper for background
Brown paper for surround
Cake board or alternative mount 12in by
    9$\frac{1}{2}$in
1$\frac{1}{4}$yd braid to frame (optional)
Scotch "Magic" invisible tape
Polycell wallpaper paste
Copydex fabric adhesive
Evo-stik clear adhesive

Method: Trace the whole figure on to medium-weight Vilene, *except* for the left arm–follow the line A-A at the shoulder, and the broken line indicating the side of the skirt: ignore the broken lines indicating the collar and cuff. Now trace the left arm separately. Cut both pieces out very carefully: it is best to cut out the section at the back of the neck with a sharp craft knife, so it may be wiser to ask a grown-up for help.

Cut away the head and shoulders along the neckline A-B. Cut off the arms along the lower edge of each sleeve. Cover these three pieces with black paper in the usual way.

Now cut the bodice and right arm away from the skirt along the waistline C-C, and divide the overskirt and underskirt along D-D.

Cover the bodice and right arm, the left arm, and the overskirt with green fabric.

Cover the underskirt with deep golden-yellow fabric.

Tape all the pieces together again, adding the left arm last, and sticking the lower part down over the skirt as shown on the pattern, with the tip of the hand overlapping the underskirt.

Trace the collar, in two pieces, on to light-weight Vilene. Stick or stitch the outer edge of your lace along the lower edge of the collar, slightly overlapping: allow the cut ends to overlap at each shoulder. Trim the inner, straight edge of the lace where the collar pieces narrow towards the centre, and then gather and stick the lace evenly to the Vilene. Add another layer of lace half-way up the wider part of the collar, if necessary, and turn the surplus at the top and sides neatly round to the back and stick. Then stick the two collar pieces into position on the figure, following the neckline.

Cut two pieces of lace for cuffs, as indicated on the pattern, and stick over the arms, the top edge following the line of the lower edge of the sleeve.

Stick a length of greenish-gold braid over the waistline (C-C).

Trace the sleeve bows on to light-weight Vilene: then trace the outlines through to the back of the Vilene. Stick to the back of your yellow satin and, when dry, cut out. Stick into position on the sleeves, as shown.

String very tiny seed pearls round the neck and bun, anchoring the curved line in each case with a little clear adhesive "drawn" on the paper behind the pearls with the point of a pin.

Prepare your mount and paste pink paper over the entire surface for the background; add a brown surround (see pages 5 and 6).

Place the figure on the background, decide and mark position, then stick down in the usual way. (*Continued on page* 35).

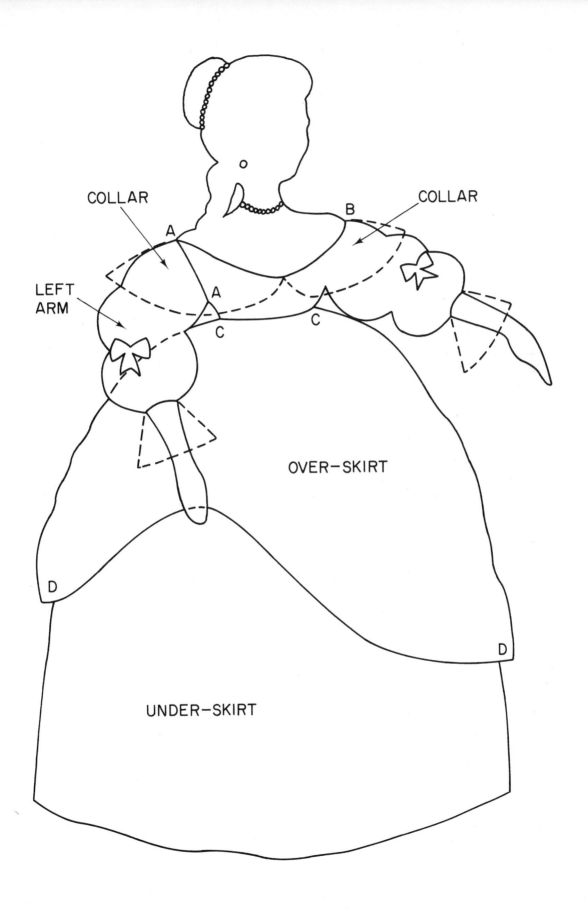

COLLAR

COLLAR

LEFT
ARM

A

B

A

C

C

OVER-SKIRT

D

D

UNDER-SKIRT

(*Left*). Henrietta Maria 1609–1669, by artist unknown. When Queen Henrietta Maria married Charles I, she brought the elegant fashions of France with her to England. She is shown here wearing an exquisite gown lavishly trimmed with pearls. The beauty of the fabric is emphasized by being left plain, to hang in softly draped silky folds which catch the play of light and shadow as the wearer moves. The low neck and high waist are bordered with pearls, and there is a tiny lace collar to match the intricately frilled cuffs on the elbow-length sleeves. Sadly, it is impossible to capture the sheer beauty of the original fabric in a collage – but you will find watered silk or moiré a very good substitute. Choose a strong, rich colour, and then make your trimmings from fine lace and tiny seed pearls.

(*Right*). Lord and Lady Clapham are a very unusual late seventeenth century lady and gentleman. Not only are they an extremely well-preserved pair of very old dolls – but they are beautifully dressed in clothes which are perfect in every detail. This makes them specially valuable to the costume historian for two interesting reasons. The first is that towards the end of the Stuart era, at the time of William and Mary, and Queen Anne, fashions changed very slowly, and then only very little: consequently, people wore their clothes out – instead of replacing them with the latest styles while their old clothes were still in good condition. This means that hardly any garments of that period have survived for us to examine for ourselves – so we have to rely on paintings for our information. And secondly, Lord and Lady Clapham are complete with all their underwear, too – and this is something which is never seen in *any* portrait!

Stick a single seed pearl into position for her earring, and an amber diamanté at the centre of the collar surrounded by a circle of tiny gilt beads to form edge of brooch, if liked.

Stick braid round the edge to frame, if required.

35

Commonwealth Severity

We have seen how feminine and charming the mid-seventeenth century fashions were, and how they flattered the Stuart ladies. But the beautiful fabrics, the lace, ribbons, feathers and jewels were also worn by their menfolk – the stylish Cavaliers–who carried their use to much greater extremes. In fact, with their flowing cloaks, vast lace collars and cuffs, plumed hats, loops and bows of ribbon decorating doublets and breeches, and the long curly hair of their wigs falling round their shoulders, the men looked extremely effeminate! This decorative taste in dress echoed the style of life at court, which was lavish and extravagant.

Then came Oliver Cromwell, and after the Civil War between the Cavaliers and Roundheads, the defeat of the monarchy. The King was beheaded, the Queen fled to France, and the country was governed by the Protectorate, under the Puritan Cromwell. Supporters of the new Commonwealth rule disapproved strongly of the be-ribboned Cavaliers in their gay clothes. And so they adopted a sober style of dress which was as different as they could make it, to emphasize the carefree style of life enjoyed by the luxury-loving Royalists.

The most extreme and serious-minded Puritans wore deliberately austere clothes made of practical, homespun fabrics in dark colours–brown, grey, purple or black. They wore high white linen collars, with no trimming, and the long sleeves had similar cuffs. Women usually wore a white apron, and their hair was hidden under a tight white cap. Both men and women wore a tall black felt hat with a brim, finished with a ribbon and buckle.

However, not everyone held such severe views, and so not everyone wore such severe clothes. The majority of Cromwell's supporters adopted the simple Puritan style of dress and sober, dark colours, but made in finer fabrics, their plain collars, cuffs and bonnets trimmed with rows of lace, copying the Royalists.

Commonwealth: 1660

Materials:
Medium-weight Vilene
Mid grey felt for top of dress
Dark grey felt for skirt
Black felt for hat
Plain white cotton for collar, cuffs, etcetera
Plain or woven white cotton for apron
$\frac{1}{2}$in wide white lace for collar and cuffs
Narrow white lace for bonnet and apron
Black Russian braid for hat-band
White Russian braid for waist-band
Silver paper or foil for buckle
Black paper for face and hands
Leaf green paper for background
Grey paper for surround
Cake board or alternative mount 12in by 9$\frac{1}{2}$in
1$\frac{1}{4}$yd braid to frame (optional)
Scotch "Magic" invisible tape
Polycell wallpaper paste
Copydex fabric adhesive
Evo-stick clear adhesive (optional)

Method: Trace the whole figure on to medium-weight Vilene, *except* for the right arm—follow the edge of the collar A-A, and the broken line indicating the side of the skirt: ignore broken line round face. Now trace the right arm separately. Cut both pieces out very carefully.

Cut away the head along the top edge of the collar, and the edge of the *hat*, so that the bonnet is included. Cut off the hands along the edge of the cuffs. Cover these three pieces with black paper in the usual way.

Now cut the top of the body away from the skirt along the waistline (B-B). Cover this whole piece—including the collar and cuff—and the right arm and cuff, with mid grey felt.

Cover the skirt with dark grey felt.

Cover the hat with black felt.

Tape the hands back into place, then join the body at the waist.

Now trace the bonnet, the two collar pieces,

the cuffs and the apron, on to medium-weight Vilene again. Cut out carefully.

Cover the bonnet, collar pieces and cuffs with plain white cotton, and the apron with either plain or woven cotton according to choice (the woven pattern of the fabric used in the illustration adds texture and interest to the collage).

Stick or stitch very narrow white lace round the inner, scalloped edge of the bonnet. Then stick the bonnet into position on the head—and stick another row of lace to the *back* of the Vilene, so that the outer edge overlaps the edge of the face as indicated by the broken line.

Tape the hat back into place round the top of the head, and join the head to the figure at the neck.

Stick or stitch the outer edge of your $\frac{1}{2}$ inch wide white lace along the lower edge of each collar piece, very slightly overlapping. Then gather and stick the top edge down neatly, trimming level at the sides. Repeat with a second row of lace overlapping the top edge of the previous one. Edge the cuffs with one row of lace only in the same way.

Stick the collar and cuffs into position on the figure.

Stick narrow white lace round the sides and bottom of the apron, sticking the inner, straight edge of the lace to the *back* of the Vilene (overlap the lace a little less at the left side—see the picture).

Stick the apron into position over the skirt. Stick white Russian braid round the waist, overlapping the cut ends at each side: take these round and stick to the back.

Tape the right arm into place (along A-A), and then stick the cuff and hand over the skirt and apron, as shown.

Stick black Russian braid round the crown of the hat as indicated by the broken line, finishing each side at the back as for the waist-band.

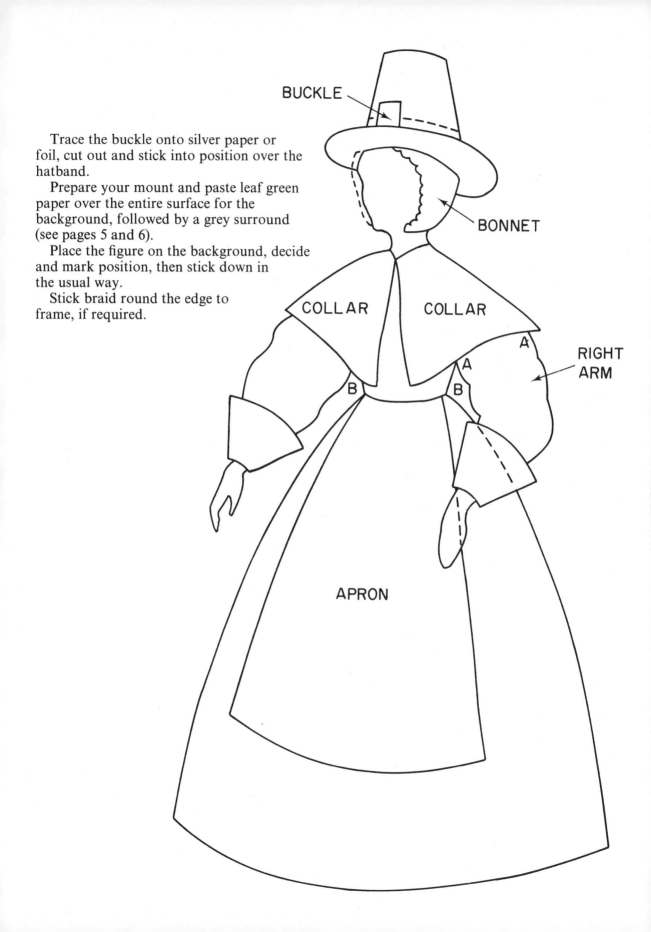

BUCKLE

BONNET

Trace the buckle onto silver paper or foil, cut out and stick into position over the hatband.

Prepare your mount and paste leaf green paper over the entire surface for the background, followed by a grey surround (see pages 5 and 6).

Place the figure on the background, decide and mark position, then stick down in the usual way.

Stick braid round the edge to frame, if required.

COLLAR   COLLAR

A

A

RIGHT ARM

B   B

APRON

Georgian Ostentation

After the sober severity of the Puritanical Commonwealth period, the Restoration of the monarchy with Charles II brought back all the frills, lace and ribbons of the Cavaliers – but with an added gaiety and abandon which tended to make men's fashions almost ridiculous. For women, the waistline dropped to its normal level, and very full skirts were worn looped back from the centre with ribbon bows to show the underskirt. Apart from this, they remained much the same – feminine and elegant, with falling lace collars, puffed and flounced sleeves and softly curled hairstyles.

Charles II had spent much of his exile in France, and French fashions strongly influenced the English court. During this time, the French court developed into a glittering world of fantastic extravagance: first Louis XIV, the "Sun King", and then Louis XV and Louis XVI, all spent vast amounts of money seeking to enjoy the pleasures of life, and outdo all their rivals with the luxury and flamboyance of the enormous court with which they surrounded themselves at their various palaces. The immoral love life of the Kings was notorious, and the ladies of the aristocracy devoted themselves with great seriousness to following the latest fashions: their toilet was their most important concern, and took hours to complete.

The French influence continued in England during the reigns of William and Mary, and Queen Anne, and still existed when the House of Hanover and its sober succession of Georges came to the throne. The exaggerated styles and over-decoration which gradually developed from the splendour of the French court once more made fashion grow stiff and unnatural. Embroidery and rich damasks and brocades became popular again, and in order to display their design to advantage, the wide skirts were held out at the sides over "panniers" – a basket-like framework tied round the waist so that it extended outwards over each hip: at the time of Queen Anne, the hoop had been re-introduced, but it grew so large that it became unpractical, resulting in the pannier style, where the dress was flat at front and back.

Gowns were extravagantly trimmed with lace, ribbons, flounces, ruching and pleats. Bows, tassels, frills, ruffles and swathed loops of ribbon appeared in abundance – and when no more decoration could be accommodated on the body, it overflowed on to the head!

High-piled hairstyles became fashionable, and these grew to such immense proportions that they soon had to be accomplished by wigs of false hair dressed over a padded frame. Large curls softened the sides and back, and hung down over the shoulders – and the elaborate completed hairdo was then covered with a fine dusting of white powder over a scented ointment called "pomatum", to give it a pale, transluscent silver-grey finish. Finally came the decoration: flowers, feathers, ribbons, jewels, ropes of pearls, lace caps, tiny straw hats and all manner of ornaments were balanced precariously atop their vast powdered wigs by ladies of fashion.

Georgian: 1770

Materials:
Medium-weight Vilene
Light-weight Vilene
Pale silver-blue and coffee brocade for gown
Deep cream fabric for undergown
Coffee brown satin or satin ribbon for bows
  on gown
Cream satin or satin ribbon for bow on head
$\frac{3}{4}$in wide white lace for wrists
Very narrow white lace for neckline
Narrow cream braid for gown
Pale coffee decorative braid for underskirt
Tiny seed pearls for hair
Clear diamanté for hair (optional)
Black paper for head and arms
Blue paper for background
Brown paper for surround
Cake board or alternative mount 12in by 9$\frac{1}{2}$in
1$\frac{1}{4}$yd braid to frame (optional)
Scotch "Magic" invisible tape
Polycell wallpaper paste
Copydex fabric adhesive
Evo-stik clear adhesive

Method: Trace the whole figure on to medium-weight Vilene, *except* for the lower part of the right arm – follow the edge of the sleeve, and the broken line indicating the side of the skirt: also ignore the bows on the sleeves and back of the head (follow line of arm or head in each case). Now trace the lower part of the right arm separately. Cut both pieces out very carefully.

Cut away the head round the neckline – A-A-A-A. Cut off the lower part of the left arm along the edge of the sleeve. Cover these two pieces, and the right arm, with black paper in the usual way.

Now cut along the front edges of the gown (A-B), and divide the undergown into two pieces at the waist.

Cover the two sides of the gown with brocade, and the bodice and skirt of the undergown with deep cream fabric.

Stick three rows of decorative braid to the underskirt, as indicated by the broken lines on the pattern.

Stick the top edge of some narrow lace along the lower edge of the head at the neckline, as indicated by the broken line: cut surplus level with edge of Vilene.

Tape the head to the bodice of the undergown. Then tape the bodice of the gown at each side, between A and the waist. Finally, join the underskirt between the two sides of the gown skirt. Tape the arms into position, and stick the right arm over the gown, as shown.

Stick narrow cream braid all round the front edges of the gown (over lines A-A-B).

Cut $\frac{3}{4}$ inch wide lace to shape for sleeve frills, following the broken lines on the pattern. Stick into position.

Trace the bodice, sleeve and skirt bows, and the two swathed pieces, onto light-weight Vilene: then trace through to the back, before sticking the right side to the back of your coffee satin. When dry, cut out and stick into position, following the pattern.

Trace the bow on the head on to light-weight Vilene – following the broken line instead of the edge of the head. Cover and cut this in cream satin as above, and stick excess to back of head (place the bow and then the figure on top of the pattern to determine the position).

Prepare your mount and paste blue paper over the entire surface for the background, followed by a brown surround (see pages 5 and 6).

Place the figure on the background, decide and mark position, then stick down in the usual way.

Stick seed pearls into position to decorate the hair, as indicated on the pattern, adding a diamanté at the top if liked.

Stick braid round the edge to frame, if required.

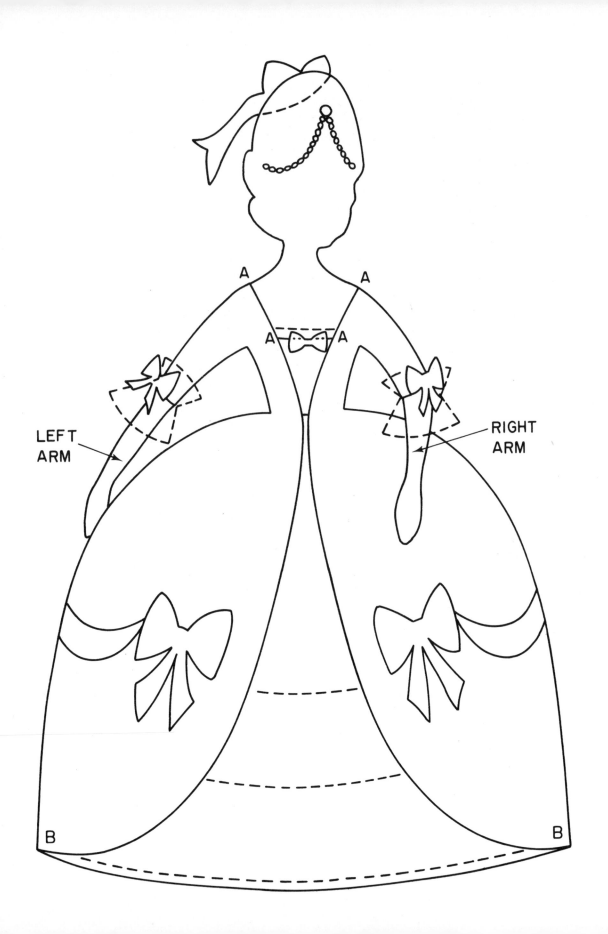

A   A

A   A

LEFT
ARM

RIGHT
ARM

B   B

(*Left*). Portrait of Queen Charlotte by Thomas Gainsborough. Reproduced by gracious permission of Her Majesty the Queen. Gainsborough's portrait of Queen Charlotte personifies the soft, graceful and utterly feminine styles which were fashionable in the later years of the eighteenth century. They reflect the extravagant, leisured life of the French court, where beauty was the criterion in all things. It was only when these charming fashions were carried to such ludicrously exaggerated extremes – by ladies determined to outdo each other in the width of their skirts, the height of their hairstyles and the variety of decoration with which they adorned themselves – that they became absurd, unflattering, and often even comical (as in the fashion plate on page 1). Queen Charlotte, wife of George III, wears a shimmering, fairytale gown of filmy fabric embroidered all over with silvery highlights. Both the underskirt and overskirt are frilled and ruched, the sleeves have deep flounces of fine lace, beneath outsize bows of broad satin ribbon echoing the one on the bodice. Her high-piled, grey-powdered wig has soft, loose curls, with ringlets at the back, and is decorated with tiny flowers.

(*Right*). The Duke and Duchess of Cumberland painted by Thomas Gainsborough. Reproduced by gracious permission of Her Majesty the Queen. Another Gainsborough lady – this time the Duchess of Cumberland, painted with her husband. Despite the shining buttons, braid and decorations adorning his well-cut jacket and waistcoat, the poor Duke finds it difficult not to be overshadowed by his elegant wife! Her beautiful, pale gown is delicately frilled and draped, falling into a train at the back – and her high wig is topped by an enormous straw hat trimmed with ribbons and flowers. Incidentally, these two pictures include another fashion which was popular at this time – the small but very lively dogs at their owners' feet!

44

45

Regency Simplicity

With the French Revolution at the end of the eighteenth century, we once more see a complete reversal of fashion. The artificial and excessively extravagant styles loved by the French aristocracy disappeared with them, and were replaced by a mode of dress which deliberately copied the classic garments of Ancient Greece.

Again France led the way, but now it was the "Directoire" fashions of Napoleon's "Empire" period, which crossed the Channel to influence a whole new way of life in English society. Architecture, furniture, decor and manners all echoed the classic Grecian simplicity of design which was all the rage at the beginning of the nineteenth century. A suggestion of this return to a more natural form of dress can be seen at the end of the previous century, when England was concentrating on developing her outstanding agricultural success: this led to a vogue for country life, and a trend towards the more simple kind of clothes which suited it.

But although ladies had already begun to dispense with their tight corsets, panniered skirts and powered wigs, the Grecian style was a complete contrast to the exaggerated fashions of only a few years before. Dresses were made in thin white or pastel-coloured cotton and muslin, instead of richer fabrics; they fitted the figure closely, the skirt falling smoothly from a very high waistline. The shoulders were completely bare, with a low neckline and tiny puff sleeves: in cold weather it was necessary to have a high neck, and long, tight sleeves below the puffed ones – but these were only added for practical purposes! Sometimes an overgown would be added too, for warmth: this had a shorter skirt – usually finished with a fringe or other decoration – so that the skirt of the dress beneath appeared below it, often ending in a train at the back.

Long, filmy scarves were draped over the shoulders – but these elegant stoles could not have given much warmth! Little or no jewellery was worn, but ladies carried tiny "Dorothy bags", enormous muffs, and parasols.

Hairstyles followed the classic Grecian line too. The hair was dressed smoothly over the head, with tiny curls across the forehead and at the nape of the neck. Indoors, flowers or feathers might be added for decoration, but out-of-doors, poke bonnets were worn, usually lavishly trimmed with ribbons and flowers or feathers.

Regency: 1810

Materials:
Medium-weight Vilene
Light-weight Vilene
White moiré or alternative fabric for dress
Pale violet satin or satin ribbon for stole and bonnet
Deep violet satin or satin ribbon for bonnet
Cream finely woven canvas, or similar alternative, for bonnet
Very narrow pale green braid for dress and bonnet
White decorative braid for skirt
Violet embroidered or artificial flowers to trim bonnet and dress
Black paper for shoulders and arms
Olive green paper for background
Deep violet paper for surround
Cake board or alternative mount 12in by 9½in
1¼yd braid to frame (optional)
Scotch "Magic" invisible tape
Polycell wallpaper paste
Copydex fabric adhesive
Evo-stik clear adhesive (optional)

Method: First of all, trace the figure on to medium-weight Vilene, *completely ignoring* the arms and stole, except for the two sections visible behind the shoulders (A and A): follow the line of the skirt through the arms and stole at each side–and also follow the line of the neck through the bow up to the lower edge of the bonnet (these are not indicated by broken lines as in previous patterns, to avoid confusion). Now trace the arms separately on to medium-weight Vilene, following the broken lines. Finally, trace the four sections of stole marked B-B, C-C, D and E on to light-weight Vilene. Cut all the pieces out very carefully.

Cut the bonnet away along the neck edge: then cut the two sections marked A, the sleeves and the bodice, away from the shoulders.

Cover this piece, and the two arms, with black paper in the usual way.

Divide the bodice and skirt along the waistline, and then cover the bodice, skirt and both sleeves with white moiré or alternative fabric (be careful not to use too fine a fabric, or the adhesive may show through–if using cotton, choose a fairly thick one: the marking in moiré makes it particularly effective and attractive, as you can see from the illustration).

Cover the six sections of the stole with pale violet satin.

Cut the bonnet into two along the edge of the brim (F-G). Cover the main part with fine cream canvas or an alternative fabric to simulate straw, and cover the inside of the brim with pale violet satin.

Placing the various pieces over the pattern to determine the exact position accurately, tape the bodice to the lower edge of the shoulders, followed by a sleeve at each side: then add the two sections of stole (A) behind the shoulders. In the same way, join the arms, followed by the four remaining sections of stole–sticking B and C where they cover the arms. Lastly, tape the skirt into position, and then stick the hands and stole down over it as shown.

Tape the two sections of bonnet together, then tape to the neck.

Trace the bonnet band and bow separately on to light-weight Vilene, then trace the outlines through to the back. Stick the right side of the Vilene to the back of your deep violet satin. When dry, cut both pieces out very carefully and stick into position on the figure.

Stick narrow pale green braid round the brim of the bonnet, beginning above the bow (point F) and taking the braid up over the join and round at the top (point G), then stick the edge to the *back* of the Vilene, so

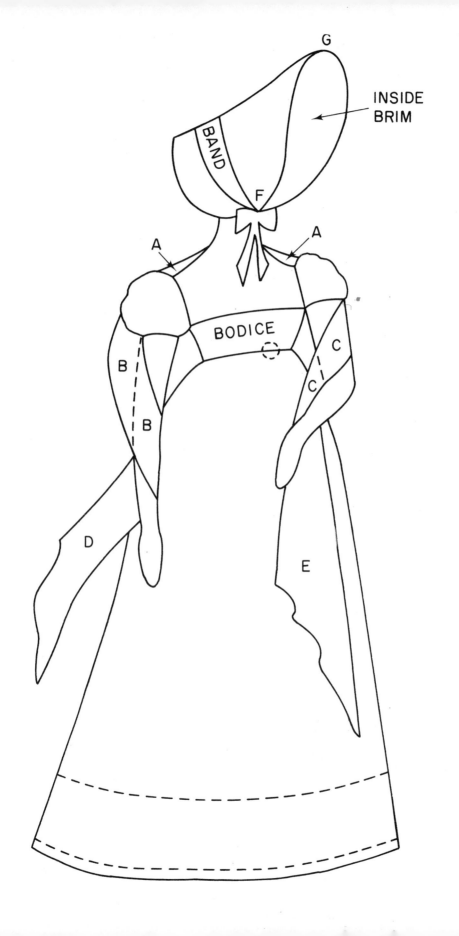

INSIDE
BRIM

G

BAND

F

A   A

BODICE

B

B

C

C

C

D

E

that it only slightly overlaps the front edge of the brim (see the illustration).

Stick the same narrow braid along the lower edge of each sleeve, and over the waist-line. Add a violet embroidered or artificial flower at the waist, as indicated.

Stick two rows of decorative white braid round the hem of the skirt, as shown.

Prepare your mount and paste olive green paper over the entire surface for the background, followed by a violet surround (see pages 5 and 6).

Place the figure on the background, decide and mark position, then stick down in the usual way.

Trim bonnet with embroidered or artificial flowers, as illustrated.

Stick braid round the edge to frame, if required.

WALKING DRESSES.

FULL DRESS.

(*Above*). A fashion plate of 1805. The two ladies on the left (yes, despite her masculine hat, it *is* a lady!) are dressed for walking, whilst the lady on the right wears evening dress. The two day outfits have their low necklines filled in, and long sleeves – the lady with the strange headgear wearing a short coat for extra warmth. For both day and evening, long, narrow stoles were very popular – and so were silk or velvet turbans decorated with plumes, like the ones illustrated here. (*Victoria and Albert Museum. Crown Copyright*)

(*Left*). The fluid lines of the Empire styles fashionable during the Regency period are clearly expressed in this youthful ball dress. It has the typically low, almost off-the-shoulder neckline and very high waist which reduce the bodice to a narrow strip between short, puffed sleeves finished with frills. The narrow skirt sweeps into fullness at the back, and is decorated with rows of pin tucks and lace flounces between clusters of artificial flowers. More flowers form part of the soft, short hairstyle, which curls prettily round her face. (*Victoria and Albert Museum. Crown Copyright*)

The winter of 1811 was most unusually cold, and for the ladies who had grimly shivered through previous years, determined not to renounce their thin fabrics, low necks and bare arms, the freezing temperature at last proved too much! After this, the extreme undress of the early years of the century gave way to warmer, more practical fashions, with long, tight sleeves, heavier fabrics which did not cling to the body, and sensible, fur-lined, hooded cloaks. Skirts became fuller, and slowly both the waist and hemline began to descend, until by 1825–30 the waist had reached its natural level, and hems once more touched the ground. (*Victoria and Albert Museum. Crown Copyright*)

Mid~Victorian Prosperity

The Industrial Revolution had a dramatic effect on English fashion. Machinery was invented which meant that cloth could be woven in vast quantities, making it much cheaper than ever before. Braids and trimmings too, could be manufactured, and so naturally fashion took advantage of these new-found opportunities. There was a prosperous new middle-class society too, so that following fashion was no longer restricted to ladies of the aristocracy. And finally, England had a young Queen, whose dresses were immediately copied by her subjects.

When Victoria came to the throne in 1837, the waistline had already dropped to its normal level, skirts had become wider, and full sleeves, high necks, shawls and capes made clothes more practically suited to the English climate. The abundance of cheap material encouraged skirts to become fuller and fuller—usually flounced—until by the middle of the century, they had to be held out over a cage-like crinoline petticoat of whalebone hoops.

As before when wide skirts were fashionable, it followed that much importance was placed on a slender waist—emphasized by a tightly fitting bodice and wide sleeves. The pointed waistline was usually accented by rows of trimming forming a V shape across the bodice, and often a V shaped neckline too—leaving the shoulders bare for evening, but filled in with a high-necked top for daytime. The bell-shaped "pagoda" sleeves revealed a contrasting puffed under-sleeve, usually ending in a frill at the wrist. Braids, fringes and buttons were used extensively to trim all garments, decorating bodices, sleeves, skirts and edging flounces—and lace was added wherever possible, particularly for evening wear.

The Victorians are remembered for their very high moral standards, and their clothes typified this in an obsessively prudish attitude to modesty: to show an ankle was outrageous, and almost every inch of the body had to be covered with layers of clothing to prevent it being exposed to view! Several starched calico petticoats, as well as one of red flannel, were worn under the skirt, and the legs were encased in long pantalettes. The hair was swept smoothly down from a centre parting to conceal the sides of the face under a demure bonnet tied securely under the chin—whilst a tiny lace cap trimmed with frills, ribbons and bows, had to be worn indoors.

However, bare shoulders and arms were permissable for evening, when dresses were even more elaborate, in delicate fabrics with extravagantly flounced skirts and sleeves, lace frills, ribbons, bows and flowers. Rosebuds were particularly popular, and were used to trim bonnets, caps and dresses for both day and evening.

Mid-Victorian: 1850

Materials:

Medium-weight Vilene
Light-weight Vilene
Deep rose fabric for dress
Deep rose satin or satin ribbon for bonnet
Pale rose satin or satin ribbon for bonnet
White woven cotton or lace for under-sleeves
½in deep white guipure lace for skirt
Very narrow white lace for neck, wrists and
  bonnet
Very narrow deep rose braid
Wider deep rose braid for hem (optional)
Pink embroidered or artificial flowers
Tiny pink beads for buttons
Clear diamanté or bead for brooch
Black paper for face and hands
Cream paper for background
Wine-coloured paper for surround
Cake board or alternative mount 12in by
  9½in
1¼ yd braid to frame (optional)
Scotch "Magic" invisible tape
Polycell wallpaper paste
Copydex fabric adhesive
Evo-stik clear adhesive

Method: Trace the whole figure on to medium-weight Vilene, *except* for the right arm–follow the edge of the trimming line (A-A), and the broken line indicating the side of the skirt: follow the broken lines through the bow, indicating the neck–but ignore those behind the bonnet and at the wrist. Trace the right arm separately. Now trace the head alone–ignoring the bonnet completely, and following the broken line indicating the back of the head: take your tracing down to the neck of the dress, ignoring the bonnet's bow and strings. Finally, trace the *outside* of the bonnet only, ignoring all broken lines. Cut all the pieces out very carefully.

Turn the main figure over and mark the lines of the trimming on the bodice and sleeve on the back of the Vilene–also the buttons. Mark the trimming line on the separate right arm in the same way.

Cut off the hands along the wrist edges. Cover these, and the separate head, with black paper in the usual way.

Cut the whole bonnet and head off the main figure in one piece along the neckline of the dress. Cover with pale rose satin.

Cover the separate outside section of the bonnet with deep rose satin.

Cut the under-sleeves away along the top edge, and cover with white woven fabric or lace.

Cut the bodice away from the skirt along the waistline (B-B-B). Cover this piece and the separate sleeve with deep rose fabric. Then divide the skirt into four layers along the lines C-C, and cover each section with the same fabric.

Tape the four skirt sections together again. Stick guipure lace trimming along the lower edge of each layer (lines C-C), adding a row of very narrow deep rose braid over the top of the lace. Stick a row of double-width braid along the edge of the hem.

Tape the hands to the under-sleeves, then stick narrow lace at each wrist, as indicated by the broken lines. Tape the under-sleeves to the sleeves.

Stick the black-covered head into position over the pale pink satin of the inside brim of the bonnet. Then stick the bonnet outside piece into position, overlapping these two pieces, outer edges level. Stick the inner edge of some lace to the back of the Vilene, so that it overlaps the back of the bonnet as indicated by the broken line.

Tape the completed head back into position at the neck of the bodice. Add a "collar" of very narrow lace at the neckline.

Tape the bodice to the skirt at the waist, and add the right arm. Stick the arm and hand over the skirt, as shown.

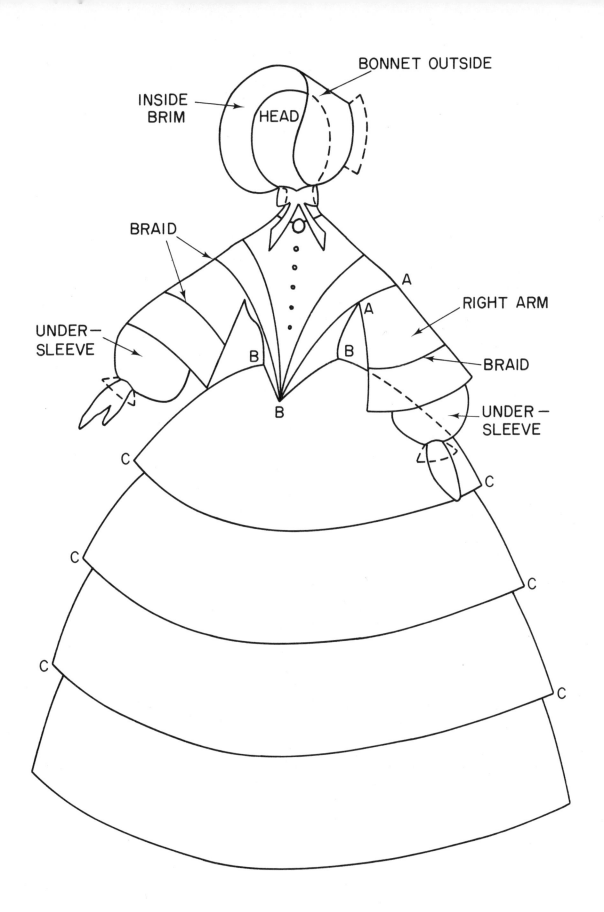

INSIDE BRIM

BONNET OUTSIDE

HEAD

BRAID

RIGHT ARM

BRAID

UNDER-SLEEVE

UNDER-SLEEVE

A

A

B

B

B

C

C

C

C

C

C

C

C

Stick rows of very narrow braid over the bodice and sleeves as indicated, and shown on the illustration: push pins through from the back to make marks indicating the correct position. Then stick a row along the waistline.

Mark the position of the buttons in the same way, and stick tiny pink beads into place as shown. Stick diamanté or a bead at the neck for her brooch.

Trace the bonnet bow on to light-weight Vilene, then turn it over and trace the outline through to the back. Stick the right side of the Vilene to the back of your deep rose satin: when dry, cut out and stick into position.

(*Right*). Mid-Victorian fashion for indoor and outdoor wear in the winter months. The visitor carries a muff in the same fur as the broad bands edging her warm, three-quarter length coat, which has a deep shawl collar and wide sleeves. It bells out from a fitted waist over her crinoline skirt, which hangs in flounces edged with fringe. Her tiny bonnet is trimmed with lace. Her friend wears a day dress trimmed with rows of ruching: the high neck is finished with a white lace collar to match the very full under-sleeves beneath the pagoda sleeves of the gown. Her cap of ribbon, lace and flowers sits well back on the crown of the head.

(*Left*). Two romantic young ladies of 1850 dressed for the ballroom. This fashion plate shows all the frills, flounces, ruching, lace, ribbons and flowers so popular during Queen Victoria's reign. The invention of machinery meant that trimmings could be mass-produced and the temptation to use them in quantity proved irresistible. Notice, however, that the girl on the left wears only a modest amount of unobtrusive jewellery – whilst the other wears none at all, preferring posies of flowers to add a natural charm to her appearance. Both girls wear their hair parted in the centre and brought smoothly down over the face and ears – just like their Queen.

Cut embroidered or artificial flowers in half and stick round the edge of the face inside the bonnet brim. Stick whole flowers to the back of the bonnet, following the illustration for guidance.

Prepare your mount and paste cream paper over the entire surface for the background, followed by a wine-coloured surround (see pages 5 and 6).

Place the figure on the background, decide and mark position, then stick down in the usual way.

Stick braid round the edge to frame, if required.

(Victoria and Albert Museum. Crown Copyright)

Late-Victorian Sophistication

As we have seen throughout the history of costume, fashions always tend to be exaggerated to a point where they are too extreme. This was the case with the crinoline, which grew so wide that it became almost ridiculous – as well as uncomfortable and unpractical. Gradually it changed in shape, becoming much flatter at the front and sides, with most of the fullness at the back. Skirts were still very full, but now they were looped back over the crinoline, so that they were smoothly draped across the front and up at the sides.

The mid-century frills, flounces, flowers, fringes, lace, ribbons and embroidery all featured in such profusion that the total effect was merely an appearance of over-fussiness, with nothing shown to advantage. But now Paris dominated the fashion scene more than ever before, and a new elegance became apparent, as gowns were designed to display the female figure in the most dignified way. Poise and erect carriage were essential, and good deportment had to be studied very seriously by ladies of fashion.

Bodices were smoothly fitted, with a high bust and a low waistline to emphasize the slender waist: sleeves were tight-fitting too, and usually ended in a decorative cuff. A high, up-standing collar closely encircled the neck on day dresses, although low necklines were still fashionable for evening.

Gradually, as this silhouette developed, the crinoline disappeared altogether – all that remained was a basket-like framework at the back, tied on just below the waist, which supported the padded "bustle". Now the skirt fitted smoothly at front and sides, with all the fullness at the back, looped up over the bustle and then falling below in a sweeping train behind. To accentuate the draped effect, dresses often had an "apron" front – as in our collage – hanging smoothly over the skirt in front and looped up at the sides.

Colours were now generally darker, and although trimming was still very important, and appeared profusely, it was used much more tastefully. Flounces, frills, pleats, bows, ribbons, braids and lace all decorated the fashions of the period, but always as a part of the design of the dress, instead of looking as if they had been added as an afterthought – just for the sake of having them!

Hairstyles were elaborate – swept to the back, following the line of the dress, and piled high, with loose curls falling down the back of the neck. Bonnets and hats were small, worn on top of the head, and elaborately trimmed.

Late Victorian: 1875

Materials:
Medium-weight Vilene
Light-weight Vilene
Dark brown fabric for the dress
Dark brown satin or satin ribbon for parasol
  and bow
Cream finely woven canvas, or similar
  alternative for the hat
½in wide cream lace for neck, wrist, parasol
  and hat
Pale coffee decorative braid for dress
Brown, golden-yellow and cream artificial,
  embroidered or lace flowers to trim hat and
  parasol
Tiny round seed pearl for ear-ring
Small oval pearl or bead for parasol (optional)
Very fine strip of split bamboo, stick, grass
  stalk or similar alternative, for parasol
  (optional)
Black paper for head and hand
Light olive paper for background
Dark brown paper for surround
Cake board or alternative mount 12in by
  9½in
1¼yd braid to frame (optional)
Black fibre-tipped pen or black ink
Scotch "Magic" invisible tape
Polycell wallpaper paste
Copydex fabric adhesive
Evo-stik clear adhesive

Method: Trace the whole figure on to medium-weight Vilene, *except* for the hand (follow the lower edge of the sleeve), the bow and streamers on the hat (follow the broken lines indicating the edge of the hat and head). Now trace the whole arm, including the hand, separately (ignore broken lines indicating cuff). Cut these two pieces out very carefully.

Cut off the head along the neck edge of the dress, and the hand from the separate arm, along the edge of the sleeve. Cover with black paper in the usual way.

Now cut the remaining figure into sections. First, cut away the bustle (A), then the upper part of the train (B) and then the lower part of the train (C). Finally, cut away the skirt. This will leave you with a piece composed of the bodice, sleeve and apron.

Cover these five pieces, and the separate arm, with dark brown fabric: if this has a noticeable vertical weave, cover the pieces so that the line of the fabric follows the arrows on the pattern.

Tape the five sections of the figure together again very carefully. Tape the hand and separate arm together again, then stick into place, over the existing shape on the figure. Tape the head to the neck, taking care to position very accurately by placing both pieces over the pattern.

Cut cream lace ¼ inch deep and stick over neck of dress, and follow broken lines for shape of cuff: stick over wrist, as indicated.

Stick pale coffee trimming over the edges of the apron, bustle and train, as illustrated.

Trace the hat (following the broken line) on to medium- or light-weight Vilene, and cut out. Cover with cream finely woven canvas or an alternative fabric. Then cut a length of cream lace ¼ inch deep, and stick the inner edge to the *back* of the Vilene, so that it overlaps the edge of the hat as illustrated. Stick the hat to the head.

Trace the bow and streamers (adding a little extra at the top of each streamer, to overlap the head) on to light-weight Vilene, then turn it over and trace the outlines through to the back. Stick the right side of the Vilene to the back of your dark brown satin: when dry, cut out very carefully and stick into position – the ends of the streamers stuck to the back of the head (place pieces over the pattern to ensure accuracy).

Trim crown of hat with flowers, as illustrated.

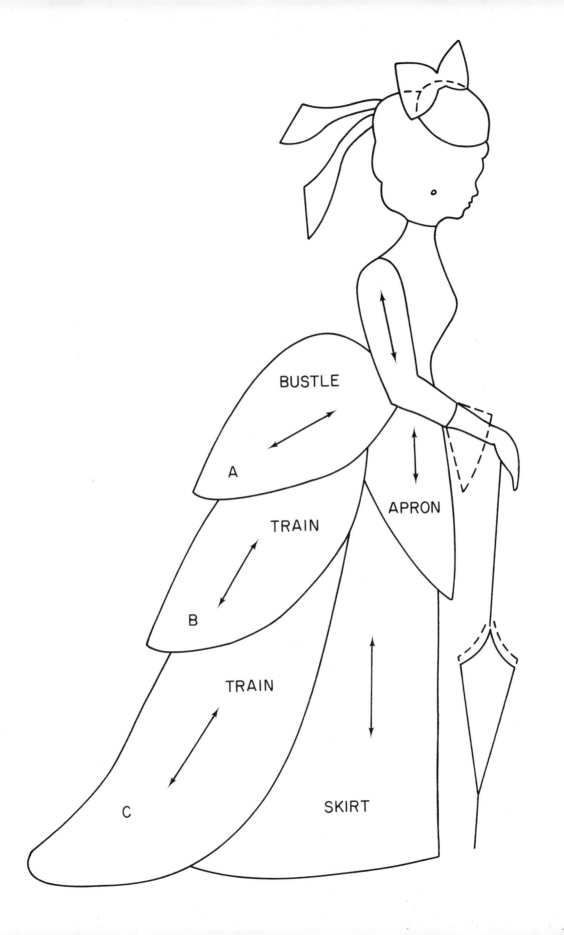

(*Above*). The art of entertaining was a carefully studied social accomplishment in Victorian times, and an elegant hostess was just as important as gracious manners and daintily prepared food and drink. These two sophisticated late nineteenth century evening dresses emphasize the graceful lines of the skirt, swept back at each side, and draped over the bustle to fall into a train behind. The front of the dress smoothly follows the line of the body from neck to hem, to produce the figure-flattering silhouette sought after by every lady of fashion. This fashion plate demonstrates how essential poise, good deportment and tightly-laced corsets were in order to wear the styles of this period successfully. (*Victoria and Albert Museum. Crown Copyright*)

Trace the parasol–ignoring the handle and tip, and the broken lines, on to medium-weight Vilene, then turn it over, trace the outline through to the back, and cover with brown satin as for the bow and streamers. Stick narrow lace round the top edges as indicated by the broken lines, as for the hat.

Prepare your mount and paste light olive paper over the entire surface for the background, followed by a dark brown surround (see pages 5 and 6).

Place the figure and parasol on the background, decide and mark position, then stick the *figure only* down in the usual way (leave the streamers until you have mounted down the main figure–it is simpler to do them separately afterwards).

Rule a black line from the palm of the hand to a point level with the hem of the skirt, for the parasol handle. Stick the satin-covered parasol over it, as the pattern. Stick an oval pearl or bead at the top for the handle (or draw a handle), and stick a very fine strip of split bamboo or similar alternative between the handle and satin (or simply leave the original black line). Trim with an artificial flower, as illustrated. Stick a seed pearl to the head for her earring, as indicated.

Stick braid round the edge to frame, if required.

The brand names of the adhesives specified in the lists of materials are those I used, to make the collages illustrated, and recommend as being very satisfactory for the specific purposes described. However, there are, of course, various equivalent products on the market, which would be equally suitable.

Most of the items used for the collages–apart from the many obvious "bits and pieces" and "odds and ends" which one always collects–were obtained from branches of the John Lewis Partnership (Oxford Street, London, W.1. and elsewhere): also The Needle-woman Shop, Regent Street, London, W.1.

(*Above*). The Bridesmaid, James Tissot 1836–1902. James Tissot painted this demure little Parisian bridesmaid in the 1880's. The top-hatted gentleman chivalrously protects her dainty forget-me-not blue dress and her charming ribbon and flower-decked straw bonnet from the rain, as she prepares to step into the carriage. She wears a tight-waisted jacket with a flared peplum over her skirt, which consists of a draped apron front caught up to form an intricate bustle at the back – over an ankle-length flounced skirt. Surely one of the prettiest dresses in our whole history of fashion!

63